BRITAIN IN OLD

AROUND
ASHFORD

STEVE R. SALTER

SUTTON PUBLISHING

Sutton Publishing Limited
Phoenix Mill · Thrupp · Stroud
Gloucestershire · GL5 2BU

First published 2006

Copyright © Steve R. Salter, 2006

Title page photograph: Upper High Street, 1954. Previously Miller & Jarvis, Geerings at 83 High Street has been a reputable name in stationery and printing since 1903 when Walter Geering founded the company. Although the retail business was taken over by Brighton firm Sussex Stationers in early 2000, the printing business still thrives at Cobbs Wood. (*Reflections/Weavers*)

British Library Cataloguing in Publication Data
A catalogue record for this book is available from the British Library.

ISBN 0-7509-4543-5

Typeset in 10.5/13.5 Photina.
Typesetting and origination by
Sutton Publishing Limited.
Printed and bound in England by
J.H. Haynes & Co. Ltd, Sparkford.

Dedicated to Mum, Dad and James

Contents

	Introduction	6
1.	Remembering How It Used to Be	7
2.	A Sentimental Journey	35
3.	Memories Are Made of These	67
4.	Everlasting Nostalgia	87
5.	Round & About	127
6.	Haven't We Been Here Before?	149
	Acknowledgements	160

Forge Lane, September 1962. This unusual view shows the rear of 33 New Rents, and its adjoining premises. (*Ken Gravett/English Heritage*)

This wonderful view shows the town in 1963 shortly before much of its redevelopment. The absence of the infamous Ringway is quite apparent here. Its construction in effect strangled the heart out of the town. Charter House now stands where the large group of trees are (top right). East Hill, the High Street and New Street were still part of the main coast to London road, and can be seen running from extreme

right to extreme left. Hayward's Garage is seen on the immediate left with the Church of St Mary the Virgin standing proudly on the right. This view illustrates a sad reminder of the vast amount of residential property and architectural treasures that were sacrificed at the end of the 1960s and throughout the 1970s. *(Simmons Aerofilms)*

INTRODUCTION

For many it's difficult to remember Old Ashford; for others it's easy. People picture the way things used to be, and many recollect with fond memories their childhood and their day-to-day lives in Ashford – and not just Ashford, but the surrounding suburbs too. Those of us who appreciate history will agree that every city, town and village in Britain has changed dramatically over the past hundred years, some more than others.

Ashford is a town that suffered during the dark days of the 1960s and '70s because of the unsympathetic manner of its redevelopment. However, it's slowly and gradually gained in many respects for the better, and now Ashfordians can safely say that the future looks bright for their once charming and peaceful little market town. There are still mixed views as to whether Ashford has any heritage or character left. The answer is YES – it has. As we speak, the local authorities and Ashford's Future Delivery Board, which are extremely conscientious in this aspect, are targeting areas of architectural and historical interest in the town, and they are being included in the enhancement, preservation and future planning of modern Ashford. Unfortunately in the real world Ashford, as it was for example in 1950, simply could not survive today. The Ringway has always had a controversial reputation, but years before its construction between 1973 and 1975, the town had to contend with gridlock in the narrow streets of the centre.

The main factors which changed the course of history for Ashford were the expansion of the railways and the establishment of a locomotive works in 1852. The population, then 4,000, soared rapidly to 6,000, which led to increased house building and marked the first steps towards Ashford's urbanisation.

A century later, in 1952, an agreement was made between Ashford Urban District Council and London County Council under which it was agreed to build 4,250 homes for the London Overspill over a period of fifteen years. So it was clear that Ashford was destined to grow in size and population. One blessing is that the town was never under-photographed during these times. We are indebted to previous generations of historians and photographers, who demonstrated a passion for recording their town in immense detail and splendour. For a town that has changed so much, decade after decade, it is necessary to take photographs to record these changes.

It is fair to assume, though, that the future planned redevelopment of Ashford will be thoughtful, and nowhere near as reckless as it was in the past. It is claimed by many local people that the authorities left themselves open to complaint and objection back in the 1960s and '70s for their reputed controversial planning, but nowadays regular public consultation with residents and businesses allows those for and against to air their views.

Around Ashford gives a fascinating pictorial tour of the town and its outskirts from the 1950s to the present day, and contains many rare photographs, showing Ashford street by street, and in overwhelming and superb detail. Many of the pictures are previously unpublished, and many haven't been seen since they were first taken. This fourth book guarantees to open the floodgates to the reader and to bring back fond memories of Ashford – the way it used to be . . .

Steve R. Salter, April 2006

1

Remembering How It Used to Be

East Hill, September 1962. It's hard to believe that this is where the Mace Lane dual carriageway now passes through towards Wellesley Road. (*Ken Gravett/English Heritage*)

East Hill, September 1962. It is barely recognisable compared with today. (*Ken Gravett/English Heritage*)

East Hill, August 1963. Further to the right, and also no longer in existence, there were four residential properties at nos 19, 21, 23 and 25 and then the premises of well-known wool staplers and dealers, Gregory & Prentis. They traded there for a number of years. As with many of the businesses of this time, their name faded away when the work started to build Mace Lane which at the time was still a dirt track. (*Ken Gravett/English Heritage*)

East Hill, August 1963. It is common knowledge that Ashford lost many public houses through redevelopment during the 1970s. But it was as early as 1960 that the Queens Head closed, to make way for alterations to the road layout where East Hill meets Hythe Road. The former hostelry remained derelict until March 1968, when it was finally demolished. Situated opposite East Hill Mill, it was in close proximity to the Star, a mere 100 yards away. Today there is still a grass verge of reasonable size where the Queens Head once stood, and one may wonder whether it needed to be demolished at all. (*Ken Gravett/English Heritage*)

East Hill, September 1962. The older white feather-edged timber mill seen from outside the familiar Gregory & Prentis premises. The remaining mill building has been for many years the site of a succession of nightclubs, the first opening in 1981 and the most recent being Liquid and Life. (*Ken Gravett/English Heritage*)

East Hill, September 1962. This splendid view shows the typical Kentish peg tile-clad timber construction of the Queens Head and adjoining properties. Fortunately today's strict guidelines prohibit the demolition of buildings of this charming character, a stance that should have been taken years ago. (*Ken Gravett/English Heritage*)

East Hill, September 1962, looking towards Hythe Road and Martyrs Field. (*Ken Gravett/English Heritage*)

East Hill, September 1962. This exceptional image depicts H.S. Pledge's six-storey East Hill Mill, Provender Mill and Mill House, ten years before it ceased to be a working mill. The landmark six-storey tower and barrel-vaulted warehouse to the right are all that remain of this once well-known site in the town, after a disastrous fire destroyed the Mill House and Provender Mill on 16 May 1974. (*Ken Gravett/English Heritage*)

East Hill, September 1962. No. 30, the premises of C. Judge, general stores, greengrocer and fruiterer, adjoin the Star Inn. Closer inspection reveals that Christina Judge, the proprietor, is advertising 'We give Express Dividend Coupons FREE', Ambrosia creamed rice priced at 1s 3d, and Prince's peas priced at 9½d. (*Ken Gravett/English Heritage*)

East Hill, September 1962. This is the shop display and frontage of Christina Judge's General Store. (*Ken Gravett/ English Heritage*)

East Hill, August 1963. Just under a year later the shop had ceased trading and the premises were boarded up. Shortly after this photograph was taken no. 30 was largely demolished, although a small section still survives adjoining the public house. The remaining site is now a car park. (*Ken Gravett/ English Heritage*)

East Hill, September 1962. The Star public house is seen here in one of its many liveries over the years. Licensees Reginald and Gladys Ormes ran the Star for over twenty years, and kept the place immaculate. In recent years the Star has suffered from frequent changes of owner and licensee, and its overall appearance has deteriorated. Even the familiar old hanging star was never replaced when it became dangerous, back in 2002. (*Ken Gravett/English Heritage*)

East Hill, August 1963. Northside at 24 East Hill, and the neighbouring Star. Note the trademark hanging star. (*Ken Gravett/English Heritage*)

East Hill, August 1963. Bridge House at no. 22 was one of Ashford School's many buildings in East Hill; Northside at no. 24, seen here on the extreme left, was another. The driveway between the two buildings once led to a quaint row of eight dwellings known as Anchor Cottages, which were sadly demolished in the late 1960s. (*Ken Gravett/English Heritage*)

East Hill, September 1962. This rare photograph is one of the very few taken of 1–8 Anchor Cottages. They were tucked away out of sight on the land behind Bridge House and Northside. A car park and sports field for Ashford School now occupy the site where these beautiful cottages once stood. (*Ken Gravett/English Heritage*)

East Hill looking towards High Street, August 1963. These two splendid views show East Hill as many old Ashfordians fondly remember it. They were taken within 50 yards of each other, and illustrate every detail of years gone by in Ashford. Notice the old road sign. At this time there was no motorway from Ashford to London, but there is a clearly visible sign reading 'Lydd Ferryfield Airport', which had its heyday about this time. (*Ken Gravett/English Heritage*)

East Hill, September 1962. Today East Hill is largely dominated by Ashford School, but back in 1962 it was home to approximately five retail premises and two public houses. The large three-storey building to the left was, and still is, part of Ashford School known as Nightingale House, named after a former headmistress. Again, the bulldozers moved in, and the private dwellings at nos 10 and 12, together with the launderette at no. 8, were demolished in 1972. (*Ken Gravett/English Heritage*)

East Hill, September 1962. Many tend to forget that East Hill has not always been largely a school precinct. The launderette at no. 8 was owned for many years by local firm Parker Brothers, while Betty's Hairstylist was at no. 4. Rumour has it that at some point in the 1960s a murder took place above the launderette. Every building seen here was demolished in 1972. (*Ken Gravett/English Heritage*)

East Hill, August 1963. It is hard to remember the days when East Hill used to flow more or less straight through to the High Street, as today the road is severed by the Ringway and East Hill itself is a no-through-road. The two imposing buildings to the right of the Duke of Marlborough public house still remain today, and have for many years been occupied by Ashford School. The Refuge is to the immediate left of the railings at nos 5 to 7, and to the right is Brooke Place. In 2005 both buildings underwent major refurbishment as part of the amalgamation plans between Ashford School and Friars School at Great Chart. The railings can still be seen today, and are in great need of refurbishment. (*Ken Gravett/English Heritage*)

Below left: East Hill, August 1963. The Refuge doesn't look as imposing here as it does today, with the Ringway passing through where the Duke of Marlborough once stood. Watney's Beer is another name from the past that faded into history in the early 1980s. *Right:* Hoskins, newsagent and tobacconist, stood at the corner of East Hill and Station Road, with Alfred Olby Ltd, wallpaper and paint suppliers, at the corner of the High Street and Station Road. (*Ken Gravett/English Heritage*)

Wellesley Road, September 1962. In the days before the infamous Ringway, many of the main roads within the town were much narrower and were thronged with a range of business premises. Nos 13a to 15 were at the time the premises of Ashford Motor Factors, suppliers of motor and motor cycle accessories. In March 1968 a number of these buildings at the High Street end of the row were demolished for a new Pricerite store replacing the former Pearks Dairies Ltd premises, and in 1974 the remainder were demolished when construction of this section of the Ringway began. The road accessing the rear of the County Hotel and various premises in the High Street can be seen on the right. (*Ken Gravett/English Heritage*)

Wellesley Road, looking towards the junction with Somerset Road, September 1962. The vacant premises of Court Farm Dairy can be seen on the immediate left at no. 9b, displaying a TO BE LET sign by local firm Scott Kendon and Ronald Pearce at 31 High Street. The traders behind the camera at the time included Lee & Son (offices) at nos 7 to 9 and at no. 9a the Central Garage of Bligh Bros Ltd, who were Ford agents. (*Ken Gravett/English Heritage*)

Station Road, September 1962. Here we see the offices of the Ministry of Pensions and National Insurance at no. 83 (left) and Whittinghams (Kent) Ltd, wool merchants, at no. 85. The house with the bay windows on the immediate left was demolished in late 1962, together with the surrounding properties and business premises, to make way for Kent House. Incidentally the access road between the house and no. 83 was not technically known as Tannery Lane in 1962. It wasn't until 1973, when a through road was constructed over the river for the Stour Centre, that it became known as Tannery Lane. The area adjacent to The Whist and Kent Wool Growers was called The Paddocks and was home to A.J. Chalmers, wholesale grocers and confectioners, Frank Davis and Co., timber merchants stores, and Thomas R. Hills, electrical distributors, to name but a few. (*Ken Gravett/English Heritage*)

Station Road, September 1962. These are the handsome premises of the Ministry of Pensions and National Insurance. After this building was demolished, the site remained largely derelict until 1986, when a new sorting office for Royal Mail was built here, replacing their temporary base at the Drill Hall in Newtown Road. (*Ken Gravett/English Heritage*)

Station Road, September 1962. The Baptist Church and nos 6 and 8 can be seen in this view looking towards the High Street. Alfred Olby, builders merchants, can be seen on the corner of the High Street at no. 1. (*Ken Gravett/English Heritage*)

Station Road, September 1962. It is difficult to recognise, but this is where Northdown House (previously Pearl Assurance House) now stands. The only building left standing is the Baptist Church to the immediate left. At the time no. 8 was occupied by Alfred Berry the bookseller and no. 6 by Knott's shoe shop. The latter had already relocated to 51 High Street when this photograph was taken. Alfred Berry later transferred his business to 2 Godinton Road, where he traded for many years as the Bible Bookshop. (*Ken Gravett/English Heritage*)

Station Road, September 1962. Just ten years later all these quaint properties were to be demolished to widen the road for the Ringway development. (*Ken Gravett/English Heritage*)

Station Road, September 1962. The Wellesley Road section of the Ringway makes this area totally unrecognisable today. (*Ken Gravett/English Heritage*)

Station Road at its junction with East Hill and the High Street, September 1962. Left to right: Hoskins, newsagent and tobacconist, at no. 2; the memorable Tiffany's Café at no. 3; County Market Stores, grocers, at nos 5, 7 and 9; J. Grout, estate, travel and shipping agents; and the butchery department of County Market Stores at nos 17–21. (*Ken Gravett/English Heritage*)

East Hill, September 1962. Hoskins, one of the many newsagents and tobacconists in the town at this time, was situated at the crossroads of East Hill, Wellesley Road, High Street and Station Road. Many will remember its corner position and entrance looking up the High Street. Hoskins, too, was to fall foul of the redevelopment plans. It was demolished in 1972 to allow Station Road to be widened for the Ringway scheme. (*Ken Gravett/English Heritage*)

High Street, at the junction with East Hill, September 1962. Wellesley Road and the Duke of Marlborough public house are on the right. (*Ken Gravett/English Heritage*)

REMEMBERING HOW IT USED TO BE

High Street (lower), September 1962. Here we see Lee & Son, pictured from Station Road, with the County Hotel to the left and the vacant premises of the former Pearks Dairies Ltd store at 2 High Street. Note the policeman standing outside the furnishers; it is rumoured that this was a regular observation point for officers on the beat, perhaps to catch the 'boy racers' of the day. It seems he was out of luck on this particular day, as the town appears deserted. (*Ken Gravett/English Heritage*)

High Street (lower), September 1962. Many Ashfordians will remember the smart premises of Lee & Son, home furnishers and removal contractors, at nos 4 to 8. They traded in the town from 1868, and at one time also had premises in Wye as well as other sites in Ashford. They finally left the town in 1967, but continued to trade for a short time from their Wye site. The High Street site was demolished in March 1968, to be replaced by a new Pricerite supermarket. (*Ken Gravett/English Heritage*)

High Street (lower), September 1962. For many years the County Hotel at no. 10 was one of the best-known hotels in the town, and it gained a good reputation. It also offered a 'sprung' dance floor in its ballroom at the rear of the premises. It was said to be one of the best in Kent in its day. Formerly known as the Fernley Commercial and Temperance Hotel, the County gradually deteriorated, partly because of a succession of short-term owners. Then in 1998 the Potters Bar chain J.D. Wetherspoon turned the ageing hotel into a music-free public house and restaurant, but the upstairs rooms are not used. (*Ken Gravett/English Heritage*)

High Street, September 1962. Another splendid picture of the County Hotel at 10 High Street. Perhaps that is the landlord standing in the doorway, taking a breather. (*Ken Gravett/English Heritage*)

High Street (lower), September 1962, looking towards Station Road. The vacant premises of Handover Brothers, outfitters, are at no. 3, with Rediffusion (South East) Ltd on the upper floor at no. 3a. All of the buildings seen here were demolished in 1970 to make way for Pearl Assurance House. (*Ken Gravett/English Heritage*)

High Street (lower), September 1962. The charming premises of Alfred Olby Ltd, builders merchants and ironmongers, at 5 High Street had previously been a public house by the name of the Royal Oak, where it is reputed that corn dealing took place. Alfred Olby acquired the premises in 1936, and traded there until it was demolished in 1970. No. 5 had also previously been occupied by Lee & Son, who were for many years situated at 2, 4 and 8 High Street. (*Ken Gravett/English Heritage*)

High Street (lower), September 1962. Another view of Alfred Olby's High Street premises. The Ashford Co-operative Society's grocery premises can be seen on the immediate right. (*Ken Gravett/English Heritage*)

High Street (lower), September 1962. These two lovely old buildings were also lost to the bulldozers in the 1970s. Florifruit, florists and nurserymen, used to occupy no. 13, roughly where Straws hardware shop now stands. Next door Soundcraft traded at no. 15, approximately where the Codfather take-away now stands (formerly Mealtime, owned by Barry Woodward), and the Household Bank (previously Abbey National) stands where Keith R.A. Skinner, optician, once traded at no. 17a. (*Ken Gravett/ English Heritage*)

Nos 13–17a High Street (lower), September 1962. Note the photogenic dog just creeping into view in the extreme bottom left-hand corner. (*Ken Gravett/ English Heritage*)

High Street (lower), September 1962. This splendid view shows one of the town's many reputable grocers, C.F. Hutson at no. 19. It was run for a number of years by Mr A.G. Morris and his son-in-law, who specialised in high-class foods and offered over sixty types of cheese. In 1974 this traditional grocer closed to make way for Ashford's first Wimpy restaurant and take-away, which has only recently closed in 2006. (*Ken Gravett/English Heritage*)

High Street (lower), September 1962. From left to right: J. Ingall & Son, chemists, at no. 42; Photocraft (Kent) Ltd, photographic dealers, at no. 40; Photocraft (Kent) Ltd, tape recorders, at no. 38; E. Beasley & Son, dyers and cleaners, also at no. 38; B.J. Marsh, corn and seed merchants, at no. 36; the Co-op tobacconist at no. 34, with the Ashford Labour Party Offices above; and Bateman, optician, at no. 32. Bateman's is the only one still trading in 2006. (*Ken Gravett/English Heritage*)

High Street (lower), September 1962. These two tile-hung properties still survive today. In 1962 no. 32 housed the radio and television department of Ashford Co-operative Society Ltd, and no. 34 a tobacconist which was also owned by the Co-op. Cllr Allen Wells and his wife Christine lived with their children above no. 34, and they always seemed to have colds. When Cllr Elsie Mayhew looked into the matter, the Wellses told her it was because the property was damp. So Cllr Mayhew moved them to another property, which they still occupy to this day, and their colds were cured. (*Ken Gravett/English Heritage*)

High Street (lower), September 1962. B.J. Marsh, corn and seed merchants, occupied no. 36 for many years and E. Beasley & Son, dyers and cleaners, shared no. 38 with the tape recorder department of Photocraft, whose main shop was next door at no. 40. (*Ken Gravett/ English Heritage*)

High Street (lower), September 1962. The classical-styled frontage shown here disguises a lovely old Kent pegged cottage, which can be seen from the rear in St Johns Lane. In 1962 the Westbourne Park Building Society occupied no. 25, which was also the district offices for Kent County Council's Building and Health department. To the left of no. 25 the Bon Bon snack bar and restaurant is seen in its heyday at no. 23, with Gizzi's restaurant further along at no. 29. (*Ken Gravett/English Heritage*)

High Street (lower), September 1962. From left to right: Globe Art, wallpaper and paint suppliers, at no. 21; the Bon Bon snack bar at no. 23; Westbourne Park Building Society (centre) at no. 25 and Gizzi's restaurant at no. 29. (*Ken Gravett/English Heritage*)

High Street (lower), September 1962. No. 31 has seen many changes in its life. Once an inn called the Ounces Head, by 1962 it was divided into three businesses. The larger part of the building, known as St John's Chambers, has been an estate agency for over forty years. Originally Scott Kendon and Ronald Pearce, and latterly Scott and Kendon, it merged with the Halifax group in 1988. The respected Ashford and Kent historian/writer Richard Filmer worked there from 1963, eventually becoming a partner. Kingsfield Bakeries Ltd are seen here occupying what is now part of the Halifax, together with the Victoria Wine Co., wine, spirit, beer and 'Cyder' merchant (previously Fendall's), on the left. The renowned Gizzi's restaurant is on the left. Many will remember the Gizzis for their high standards and their immaculate restaurant. (*Ken Gravett/English Heritage*)

High Street (lower), September 1962. No. 31 is alongside the Odeon (now a Mecca Bingo Hall). The passage to St Johns Lane and Vicarage Lane car park can be seen between no. 31 and the Odeon at no. 36. Note the direction of traffic in the High Street at this time. (*Ken Gravett/English Heritage*)

High Street, September 1962. Generations of housewives will fondly remember Henry Headley's grocer's shop at 46 High Street. It served the town for over 128 years, 118 of them from the same premises, and the business was renowned for its high standards. Founded by Henry Headley, it was the last traditional grocer's shop trading in the town when it closed in 1976. Henry Headley's two sons Burgess and Herbert started what was (and continues to be) a successful printing firm over his grocer's shop when they were just 15 and 18 years old respectively. Eventually no. 46 became Headley Brothers retail stationers in 1978 after moving up from 36–38 High Street. The retail stationery business eventually closed in 1988, and it is now a McDonald's outlet. (*Ken Gravett/English Heritage*)

High Street (lower), September 1962. These fantastic pictures show the heart of the town, when Ashfordians had a selection of specialist trades to choose from. The Chocolate Box, confectioners, newsagents and tobacconist, have been trading from no. 48 for over forty years. Above, on the upper floor, Redman's had their publishing office, together with Birlings (Kent) Ltd, the events organiser and contractor. Many locals will remember Redmans for their yearly production of 'Day by Day' street directories, which in 1962 cost 8s 6d. Further along at no. 50 were butchers J.H. Dewhurst Ltd, a name which largely disappeared from Kent in the late 1980s. Finally Boyd's radio and television dealers occupied no. 52 before Stranges, family wear and school wear, moved in from Bank Street where the Woolwich Building Society now has its premises. (*Ken Gravett/English Heritage*)

High Street, looking towards North Street, September 1962. Previously Coulthard's and then the Fifty Shilling Tailors, the attractive corner building at no. 54 was for many years the home of John Collier, gents outfitters. Many will remember the company slogan, 'John Collier, John Collier, the Window to Watch', and also their traditional high-quality tailoring. On the upper floor of no. 54 Ashley Russell Ltd, milliners and costumiers, also had a popular café until the 1950s. (*Ken Gravett/English Heritage*)

Lower High Street, looking towards Middle Row, September 1962. This picture was taken from outside 46 High Street. The upper High Street can be seen in the background (right). (*Ken Gravett/English Heritage*)

No. 54 High Street, at the junction with North Street, September 1962. The Saracens Head Hotel is on the immediate left. (*Ken Gravett/English Heritage*)

2

A Sentimental Journey

No. 2 North Street, September 1962. These are the delightful premises of Ashley Russell Ltd, milliners and costumiers, who also ran a first-floor café some years back. The interior reveals many charming features, including an old Wrights fireplace, a dumb waiter and a rounded balustraded opening looking down to the ground floor. All these features have been sympathetically preserved by the new proprietors, the Merchant Chandler. Ashley Russell's closed in 1980 after more than thirty-five years in the town. (*Ken Gravett/English Heritage*)

The Lord Roberts public house, North Street, September 1962. (*Ken Gravett/ English Heritage*)

North Street, September 1962. This is Denne's yard, behind 6–10 North Street, with the old printing and grocery warehouse in Headley's yard behind 46 High Street. The original seed and corn merchants' premises, far left, had to be demolished after a huge blaze destroyed 75 per cent of the original building. Now refurbished and rebuilt, nos 6–10 are the home of Yeung's Oriental Buffet restaurant. (*Ken Gravett/English Heritage*)

Park Street, September 1962. The popular Lord Roberts hostelry (previously the Red Lyon), in North Street is seen in this splendid view taken from Park Street. Jackson's gentlemen's hairdresser just creeps into view on the right. (*Ken Gravett/English Heritage*)

North Street, looking towards the High Street, September 1962. Another view of the Lord Roberts public house. (*Ken Gravett/ English Heritage*)

No. 14 North Street, September 1962. The attractive North Street shop of W.H. Gibbs is seen here, with its lovely window-boxes and superb window displays. (*Ken Gravett/English Heritage*)

North Street, September 1962. This nostalgic view of North Street illustrates how it looked before it was severed by the Park Street service road installed in 1974. The premises of W.H. Gibbs Ltd, house furnishers and removal contractors, can be seen here at no. 14, but they also occupied at least two other premises in High Street and Hempsted Street. The Lord Roberts public house is further along, opposite the junction with Park Street, and the tall building further along on the left was for many years the premises of T. Denne & Sons Ltd, corn and seed merchants, at nos 8 and 10. (*Ken Gravett/English Heritage*)

North Street, September 1962. Here we see the premises of E.J. Price, optician, and John Hogbin, estate agent, at nos 7 and 5 respectively. Incidentally the premises of E.J. Price are some of the oldest in Ashford. (*Ken Gravett/English Heritage*)

North Street, September 1962. This is another fascinating view, showing the variation of buildings in North Street. For many years the top windows in the front elevation of no. 9 were actually dummy windows, indicating that the building had been altered during in its lifetime – quite a common practice in many Georgian buildings. (*Ken Gravett/English Heritage*)

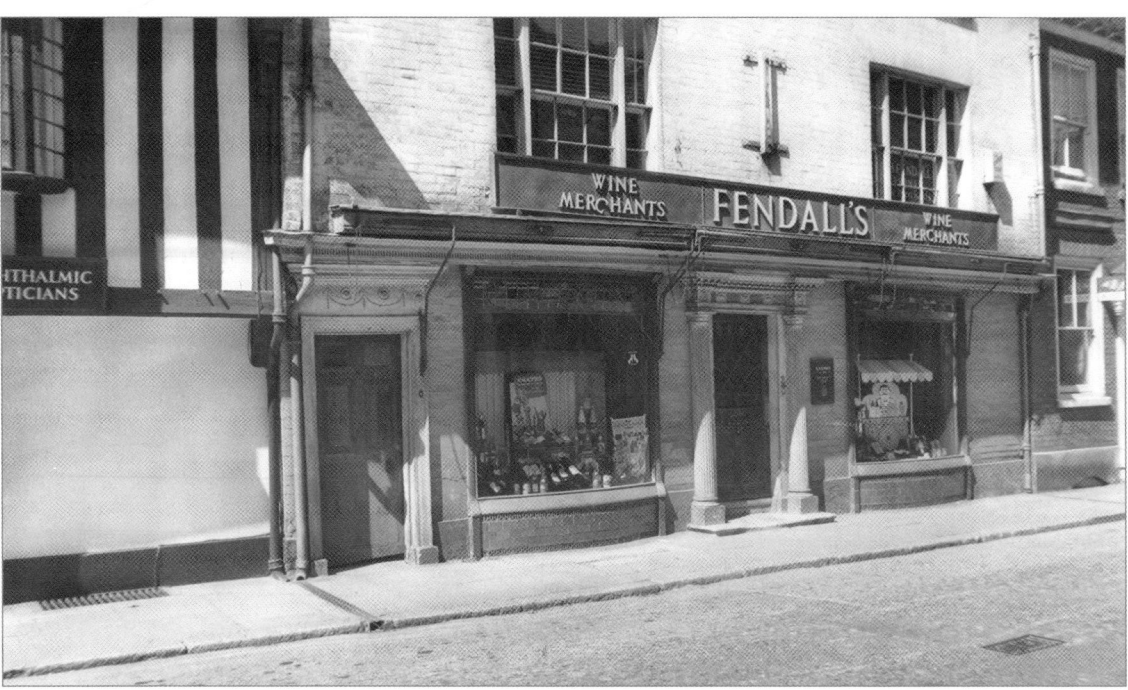

North Street, September 1962. At about this time there was a proposal to demolish the numerous historic properties at the north end of North Street to allow redevelopment of the area. Thankfully the proposal was refused, and the street is now part of a central conservation area. K.H. Fendall, wine merchants, can be seen at no. 9; for many years they also traded at 31 High Street alongside Scott Kendon and Ronald Pearce, estate agents. The double shop front (pictured) is almost identical to that of 31 High Street, and is said to have been designed by the same architect. Charter Consolidated refurbished no. 9 and its neighbouring properties between 1972 and 1975. (*Ken Gravett/English Heritage*)

North Street, September 1962. At this time the handsome premises at no. 11 were occupied by C. Jenner & Son Ltd, builders, who are still in business trading from Folkestone. More recently the premises have been occupied by Eurotunnel Developments Ltd. (*Ken Gravett/English Heritage*)

North Street, September 1962. At this time the A28 Canterbury Road/North Street was still a traffic thoroughfare. The buildings adjacent to the North Street Hall (left) are no longer in existence, having been demolished to make way for the Ringway. (*Ken Gravett/English Heritage*)

Nos 22–28 North Street, September 1962. They look not dissimilar today. (*Ken Gravett/ English Heritage*)

North Street, September 1962. The familiar North Street Hall, also known as the Masonic Hall, was at 32 North Street. Sir John Furley, the famous philanthropist and founder of the St John Ambulance Brigade, was born at no. 32, which escaped demolition in 1973 although the adjoining buildings were demolished for the Ringway construction. (*Ken Gravett/English Heritage*)

North Street, September 1962. Further along at no. 13 were the premises of Jackson & Jackson, chartered architects and surveyors, who were well known locally and undertook many projects in and around Ashford. The premises were taken over by Harrison Clague, architects, in the 1970s, with part of the building occupied by the reputable Dresden hairdressers until the 1980s. Clague's, as they are now known, are still trading here in 2006. (*Ken Gravett/English Heritage*)

North Street, September 1962. Another view of no. 13, this time looking towards the junction with Park Street. (*Ken Gravett/English Heritage*)

North Street, September 1962. This rare photograph depicts the house and premises of Dr A.V.R. Don, physician and surgeon, and Dr J.G. Elliott, physician. These doctors treated scores of Ashfordians over the years in this once-familiar property with substantial grounds beyond the substantial wall. The house was demolished in late 1969, and for many years a car park replaced it. Today the site is occupied by a number of premises including Barclay's Business Centre and the Ashford offices of the Kent Messenger Group. In the top picture, Canterbury Road leading towards Kennington can be seen in the distance. (*Ken Gravett/English Heritage*)

Middle Row, September 1962. At this time Sercombe's men's and school outfitters were in their prime, and had occupied nos 1a and a further building at no. 12 for over thirty years. This was a popular view for postcards. When Sercombe's relocated, no. 12 became the home of Davies and Tate, replacement window suppliers, in the 1980s. The business disappeared in the 1990s (by which time it was based in North Street) after the untimely death of the proprietor. (*Ken Gravett/English Heritage*)

No. 13 Middle Row, September 1962. Another much-photographed building, which at the time was occupied by Scott's dyers and cleaners. For the past twenty years the Carvery has served thousands with quality foods and tasty pastries. (*Ken Gravett/English Heritage*)

Middle Row, looking towards the Lower High Street, with Churchyard Passage on the right, September 1962. This is one of Ashford's historical gems. Marjorie Smith's needlework and wool shop is on the left. (*Ken Gravett/English Heritage*)

Middle Row, September 1962. This quaint passageway through Middle Row, in the heart of the town, is largely unchanged today. The popular Man of Kent public house, at nos 8–9, is on the left, together with Leaver's confectioners and tobacconist at no. 1b, which still trades under this name today. The premises of Marjorie Smith's popular needlework and wools shop is at nos 10–11. (*Ken Gravett/English Heritage*)

Middle Row, September 1962. The Mocha Bar is on the left, with Doughty's tobacconist's on the right. At this time Doughty's premises was divided into two, the other half being for many years occupied by Bartlett and Best, saddlers. Doughty's also had premises at 4 New Rents. The traffic sign gives clear evidence of the town's pre-pedestrianisation status. (*Ken Gravett/English Heritage*)

Middle Row, September 1962. The church of St Mary the Virgin is in the background. Leaver's is seen again, this time on the left, together with Marjorie Smith's shop. The premises of wine and spirit merchant George Prentis can be seen in the distance (right) at 57 High Street; it was one of several off-licence traders in the town back in the 1960s. (*Ken Gravett/English Heritage*)

Middle Row, September 1962. The charming and picturesque premises of the Mocha Bar are reputed to have served as a market hall many years ago. The building is particularly noted for its unusual decorative plasterwork known as pargetting, which was carefully repaired and reapplied to its original design in 1982. There was always an element of danger for diners on the first floor as double-decker buses negotiated their way from North Street past the historic building. (*Ken Gravett/English Heritage*)

Above left: Middle Row, September 1962. No. 4, once home to the familiar butchers Waghorne, is here occupied by Ashford florist and fruiterer W. Trice, who also had premises at 18 Bank Street until the early 1980s, when the florist was taken over by Lesley's. The much-photographed premises in Middle Row now houses estate agents Miles and Barr, after being home to the PDSA charity shop for over fifteen years. (*Ken Gravett/English Heritage*)

Above right: Middle Row, looking towards the Odeon, in the lower High Street, September 1962. (*Ken Gravett/English Heritage*)

Right: Middle Row, September 1962. The greatly missed and fondly remembered ironmongers and cutlers C.W. Dixon & Co. were located at 7 Middle Row. By the time they closed in the late 1970s, they had managed to notch up over seventy-five years' trading in the town. No. 7 subsequently housed a ladies' clothing shop and Thresher's off-licence, but in the mid-1980s it became part of the well-established Man of Kent public house, making the popular hostelry much bigger. (*Ken Gravett/English Heritage*)

Middle Row, September 1962. These two views show the shop's familiar frontage and the unusual jettied elevation at the churchyard side of the premises. In the years before the upper elevation was tiled, the name C.W. Dixon was sign-written between the windows, as can be seen on many old postcards. (*Ken Gravett/English Heritage*)

High Street (middle), looking towards the upper High Street, September 1962. These wonderful buildings, some of which are still in existence today, illustrate some more familiar names of the past. Knott's shoe shop, previously located at 6 Station Road, is seen here in its new premises at 51 High Street. The shoe shop closed in the late 1970s and for many years Baldwins travel agency occupied the premises. At no. 53 was Harold Rabson, watchmaker and repairer, who continued trading until 1992, but the fascinating toy shop next door at no. 55, also called Rabson's, closed in the mid-1970s and was taken over by the Wright Brothers' sports shop. (*Ken Gravett/English Heritage*)

High Street (middle), September 1962. At this time the High Street was a charming and narrow street! (*Ken Gravett/English Heritage*)

High Street (middle), September 1962. Ashford really was a peaceful and prosperous little market town, and boasted quaint streets with a range of historic buildings. (*Ken Gravett/English Heritage*)

No. 63 High Street, September 1962. This beautiful old building (centre) is said to be one of the oldest in Ashford. In 1962 it housed the well-known ladies' costumier Peggy Tyler, but nowadays it is the successful Chilli Bite South African takeaway and restaurant, owned by Robert and Tania Levin. (*Ken Gravett/English Heritage*)

High Street (middle), looking towards the lower High Street, September 1962. (*Ken Gravett/English Heritage*)

High Street (middle), looking towards the lower High Street and churchyard, September 1962. (*Ken Gravett/English Heritage*)

High Street (middle), September 1962. Still unspoilt, this part of the High Street is a favourite with those who have a passion for history and architecture. (*Ken Gravett/English Heritage*)

High Street (middle), looking towards the upper High Street, September 1962. This charming but narrow roadway runs alongside Middle Row and has always needed careful negotiation by the beer drays delivering to the Man of Kent public house. (*Ken Gravett/English Heritage*)

High Street (middle), September 1962. Here we see the familiar premises of the *Kent Messenger*, which traded here until the late 1970s. For over a hundred years this popular newspaper has kept the Kentish people up to date with a whole range of issues and subjects within their county. The proprietors bought up many of the local newspapers over a period of forty years, including the already established *Kentish Express–Ashford and Alfred News*, *Ashford Advertiser* and *Tuesday Express*, and the paper continues to excel countywide and locally under the helm of young editor Leo Whitlock. It is said that the paper's plate-glass negatives were stored in the attic of no. 69, and their weight was enough to make the ceiling beneath bow. Next door at no. 71, Grigg's (Hythe) Ltd was the last traditional fishmonger in the town; it closed in the 1990s, to the distress of local fish lovers. (*Ken Gravett/English Heritage*)

High Street (middle), adjacent to Kings Parade, September 1962. Peggy Tyler, ladies' costumier, was at no. 63; the Paradise Restaurant (previously Wrens) at no. 65; Bournes, bakers and pastrycooks, at no. 67; Kent Messenger Newspapers at no. 69; Grigg's, fishmongers, at no. 71 and Walter & Son, shoe retailers, at no. 73. Dixon's ironmongers, visible on the extreme left, was situated in Middle Row, and at one point also had premises in Tufton Street (currently Smart Cartridge). (*Ken Gravett/English Heritage*)

High Street (middle), September 1962. The wonderful old premises of Worger & Co. at 75 High Street will always be remembered for their fascinating interior, and the aroma that came from the store when one ventured inside. One of a number of corn and seed merchants within the town, Worger & Co. traded in this, one of the oldest buildings in Ashford, for over thirty years. Worger's closed in the late 1980s and the premises became a discount shop, but the interior stayed the same and even the aroma lived on. No. 75 is now occupied by the Nationwide Building Society. (*Ken Gravett/English Heritage*)

High Street (middle), September 1962. This is another superb view of Worger's premises, with the private entrance to Bull Yard to the right of their shop front. Achille Serre Ltd, the well known dyers and cleaners, can be seen to the right at no. 77. (*Ken Gravett/English Heritage*)

High Street (middle), September 1962. The Saracens Head Hotel at no. 56 was a well known hostelry dating back to at least 1478 and enlarged in 1862, stretching along North Street and backing on to Park Street. The extensive building was demolished in 1966 to make way for a new self-service supermarket for national chain J. Sainsbury. The supermarket, constructed by local firm C.I. Epps, opened in 1967 and was then state of the art in its construction. (*Ken Gravett/English Heritage*)

High Street (middle), September 1962. The Saracen's Head seen from Kings Parade, showing its immaculate appearance and prominent site on the corner of High Street and North Street. One of the best known Kentish grocers of the era, Vye & Son, can be seen on the left at no. 58. (*Ken Gravett/English Heritage*)

Bank Street, September 1962. Just behind 83 High Street were the tiny premises of Bodsham Farm Shops Ltd, which traded for many years from 1a Bank Street. On the extreme left is the National Provincial Bank at no. 2a; this was a branch of the National Westminster Bank until 1992. The handsome building which served as a post office at the turn of the nineteenth century was also the offices of the Ministry of Fuel and Power, and also the District Inspector of Quarries and Mines. (*Ken Gravett/English Heritage*)

High Street (upper), at the junction with Bank Street, September 1962. These lovely old timber-framed buildings still grace the town today. Back in 1962 they were much more divided than they are today, as illustrated in this and the following picture. No. 83 is particularly interesting in that it has a scrolled and scalloped corner just below roof level. There are two other buildings in the town that boast this unusual architectural feature: 39–41 Bank Street, which was for many years Burrows & Co., estate agents, and 13 New Street, the premises of A. Sellers & Son, butchers. All three properties may have been constructed by the same builder, but this is difficult to prove. (*Ken Gravett/English Heritage*)

High Street (upper), September 1962. This splendid view shows the occupants of nos 83 to 87 at this time. From left to right: Hepworths Ltd, outfitters; the Maypole Dairy (which was temporarily vacant) at no. 83a; Clement Clarke Ltd, optician, at no. 85; Flinn & Son Ltd, dyers and cleaners, at no. 85a; and Brighter Homes, wallpaper and paint suppliers, at no. 87. The premises of the Commercial Union Assurance Co. at nos 89–91 just creep into view on the right. (*Ken Gravett/English Heritage*)

High Street (upper), September 1962. A nostalgic view showing 83a–93 High Street in the days when the High Street was still a through road between the coast and London, and buses used to stop outside Woolworths in the foreground. This area is now extensively pedestrianised, which makes the street look much smaller, and seats and trees have been introduced. (*Ken Gravett/English Heritage*)

High Street (upper), September 1962. The handsome premises of the Commercial Union Assurance Co. Ltd at nos 89–91 stood next to a footpath that at one time led to Godinton Road, and the outfitters Lewis & Hyland at no. 93. The building had been home to a number of businesses over the years, including Vines, estate agents; Mace Windsor, solicitors, and Roselodge Kitchens, to name but a few. In the early 1980s nos 89–91 were extensively rebuilt, but retained the original façade by Coombs of Canterbury. Today the Body Shop and Starbucks occupy the ground floor, but the offices above remain vacant. (*Ken Gravett/English Heritage*)

High Street (upper), September 1962. The imposing premises of the Commercial Union Assurance Co. seen from another viewpoint. (*Ken Gravett/English Heritage*)

High Street (upper), September 1962. Here we see a fabulous selection of some of the town's lost trades. From left to right: R. & L. Hogg, grocers, at no. 95; Eastmans Ltd, butcher, which was only five doors away from Brickies at no. 109; W.H. Gibbs Ltd, house furnishers and removal contractors, at nos 97–99; J. Price (Ashford) Ltd, watchmaker and jeweller, at no. 101; L. Burch, cycles and electrical goods, at no. 103; and Courts, furnishers, at no. 105. The clock above the premises of W.H. Gibbs was taken down for restoration – and relocated outside the premises of the NatWest bank at 20 High Street in 1995, almost twenty years later. (*Ken Gravett/English Heritage*)

High Street (upper), looking towards Bank Street and Kings Parade, September 1962. (*Ken Gravett/English Heritage*)

High Street (upper), September 1962. The following pictures illustrate that part of the High Street that was demolished to make way for redevelopment, specifically for phases one and two of the Tufton Centre, which was renamed County Square in 1989. From left to right: F. Gutteridge, chemist, at no. 107; Brickies of Kent Ltd, butcher, at no. 109; and Frank Palmer, gentlemen's outfitter, at nos 111–113. The street narrowed here, with New Rents in the background and Castle Street on the right. (*Ken Gravett/English Heritage*)

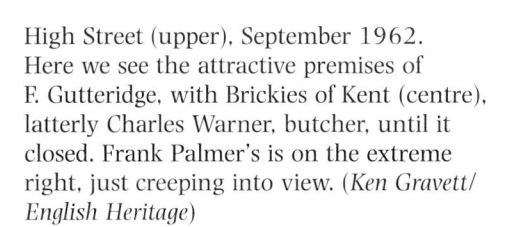

High Street (upper), September 1962. Here we see the attractive premises of F. Gutteridge, with Brickies of Kent (centre), latterly Charles Warner, butcher, until it closed. Frank Palmer's is on the extreme right, just creeping into view. (*Ken Gravett/ English Heritage*)

High Street (upper), September 1962. The well-known premises of Montague Burton, tailor, were at nos 74–76 (left), with the offices of the Prudential Assurance Co. above. Timothy Whites, chemist and hardware store, can be seen (centre) at nos 70–72, with Taylors Passage running between them. This thoroughfare was named after John Taylor, draper, who occupied the premises next door from about 1860. In 1986 nos 70–72 were demolished to make way for a new W.H. Smith. Timothy Whites had been bought out by Boots in the 1970s and nos 70–72 had therefore been Boots the Chemist for a short period. In 1978 Boots transferred to the former J. Sainsbury's store at no. 56, and their former store became Boots Cookshop until 1985. The popular George Hotel is on the right at no. 68. (*Ken Gravett/English Heritage*)

Taylors Passage, September 1962. Further towards the High Street can be seen the entrance for the offices above Montague Burton at nos 74–76 of the Prudential Assurance Co., who remained in the same premises until the early 1980s. (*Ken Gravett/English Heritage*)

High Street (upper), September 1962. It was some time before many of the larger retail chains came to Ashford but here are three of the established chains that Ashfordians will doubtless remember. From left to right: International Tea Co. Stores Ltd, grocers, at no. 92; Dolcis Shoe Co., boot and shoe retailer at nos 88–90; and F.W. Woolworth at nos 82–86. International extended their store in 1968 by demolishing the former offices of the *Kentish Express* newspaper at no. 94, but they closed in 1980. Dolcis moved to the Tufton Centre in 1975. Only Woolworths still remains in its original premises today. (*Ken Gravett/English Heritage*)

High Street (upper), September 1962. The old offices of the *Kentish Express* at no. 94, before the newspaper was taken over by Kent Messenger Newspapers. The building backed on to Park Street and apparently had a maze of cellars and open sewers underneath it, where generations of old rat-bitten newspapers were kept. When no. 94 was demolished in 1968, two carvings were discovered; originally these had formed an archway at the rear of the building, adorned with the face of a young girl. Despite extensive research, no information about the carvings has come to light. (*Ken Gravett/English Heritage*)

High Street (upper), September 1962. The opposite side of the street has also changed considerably over the past forty to fifty years, partially through redevelopment but mostly through changes in trade. Just to the right of the Castle Hotel in the distance, nos 108–110 were for many years occupied by the respected Crameri's. Many old Ashfordians still talk of the delicious pastries and the lovely restaurant, and will also recall the elegant staircase which led to the first-floor dining room. Nos 108–110 became Record Corner in 1969. Other traders included Knowles and Co. at no. 106; James & Kither (one of the last businesses in the town to use money conveyors) at no. 104; the Co-op Chemist at no. 102; Marcus's Stores at no. 100 and H. Horton & Son at nos 96–98. (*Ken Gravett/English Heritage*)

High Street (upper), September 1962. Further along from the chemist we see another two names that are no longer trading. Marcus's Army & Navy Stores, at no. 100, were always in competition with Millets of St Albans, who were in the same trade; Millets bought out Marcus's in the early to mid-1980s. Although H. Horton & Son at nos 96–98 are advertising K Shoes, it wasn't until 1966 that the store became an exclusive K Shoe shop. The offices of the *Kentish Express* newspaper and the premises of the International Stores can be seen further down on the extreme right. (*Ken Gravett/ English Heritage*)

High Street (upper), looking down the High Street, September 1962. Here, too, are more of those old names that many Ashfordians will remember. One name that disappeared in the early 1980s was Knowles & Co., house furnishers and removal contractors, and also radio and refrigerator dealers, at no. 106. At one point in their history they had at least three stores, stretching up Castle Street and New Street. After Knowles's closure, their premises at no. 106 were redeveloped to make way for the Provincial Building Society (latterly National and Provincial). James & Kither next door at no. 104 were milliners and drapers by trade, and were one of the last old-fashioned shops in the town when they closed in 1979. Their premises were to become a new store for Curry's, formerly in Bank Street. For a number of years Ashford Co-operative Chemist traded from no. 102, next door to James & Kither. (*Ken Gravett/English Heritage*)

3

Memories Are Made of These

Castle Street, September 1962. Seen here in one of its smart Shepherd Neame liveries, the Castle Hotel was one of the original coaching inns in the town. It was situated at the head of the High Street, which was at the time still a main road between the coast and London. Once known as the Kings Head, this popular hostelry underwent many changes in its history, and in later years became a venue for bikers and music. In 1996 the Castle, which was no longer a hotel, closed and was sold to the Halifax, to become their new town centre bank premises, after essential refurbishment and underpinning. (*Ken Gravett/English Heritage*)

Castle Street, September 1962. This superb view shows the Castle Hotel at no. 1, Jack Guy, pork butcher, at no. 3 and the pram and toy department of Knowles & Co. (Ashford) Ltd at nos 5–7. The junction of High Street and New Rents can be seen in the distance. (*Ken Gravett/English Heritage*)

Castle Street/New Street, September 1962. It was a sad day when the respected Ashford butcher Goddard's at 1 New Street closed, back at the beginning of the new millennium. After the untimely death of kindly gentleman Tony Ansell, the business was sold; it had been trading on the same site for over fifty years, having been established by Mr E. Goddard. The familiar rounded-corner building is seen here before the extensive alterations to the shop front carried out between 1963 and 1968. Part of the premises, known as 15 Castle Street, was occupied at this time by A.J. Hogben, grocer. Upon its closure, Goddard's was deemed the town's longest-serving quality butcher. (*Ken Gravett/English Heritage*)

New Rents, at the junction with Hempsted Street, September 1962. Frank Palmer's, gentlemen's outfitters, can be seen at the junction with Hempsted Street, with the Castle Hotel and High Street on the left-hand side. (*Ken Gravett/English Heritage*)

New Rents, September 1962. One of the most memorable businesses and department stores that came to the town in about 1838 was Lewis & Hyland. This reputable business was founded by George Alexander Lewis and started life in premises at the top of New Rents, near its junction with Forge Lane. Together with Frederick Hyland, Lewis extended into large premises stretching along New Rents at nos 9–19, and sold a whole range of quality goods, including haberdashery, millinery and drapery. These two views show the enormous building at its best, before its demolition in 1975. This wasn't the end of Lewis & Hyland though; they took two smaller units within the Tufton Centre in the same year, but sadly closed in 1982. (*Ken Gravett/English Heritage*)

New Rents, September 1962. A rare photograph showing F.G. Bradley, yeast merchant and bakers' sundriesman, at no. 33 next to R. Chandler's woodwork and model shop at no. 37. Today no. 33 is the last remaining building in New Rents, as nos 37 and 39 were demolished in 1973 to widen Forge Lane for the new Ringway. (*Ken Gravett/English Heritage*)

New Rents, looking down the narrow street towards the upper High Street, September 1962. The popular Welcome Café (centre) served good food for generations, closing in the late 1970s. In the days before B&Q and Wickes came to town, there were a number of specialist DIY stores in the town centre. Longley's at nos 12–16 was one of those traditional shops, and was in the same group of traders as Brighter Homes, Olby's and J.W. Hall. The Longley name disappeared too, in the late 1960s. (*Ken Gravett/English Heritage*)

New Rents, September 1962. At one time there were numerous butchers in town, particularly in the High Street, New Rents and New Street areas. R. Marsh & Son, pictured here at 8 New Rents, at the corner of Gilbert Road, were for many years directly opposite H.J. Davis, pork butcher, at no. 21. They continued to trade from here until the late 1970s, and more recently no. 8 became a dental practice. Jack Scott's bargain shop at no. 6 can be seen on the extreme right; this was later to become Farr's fabric shop. Mr Scott also had premises at 11 New Street. (*Ken Gravett/English Heritage*)

New Rents from Gilbert Road, showing the butchers on the right, September 1962. Lewis & Hyland's department store can be seen in the distance. (*Ken Gravett/ English Heritage*)

New Rents, looking towards the Upper High Street, September 1962. Here we see A.R. Doughty, tobacconist, who also had premises in Middle Row, and the Central Pie Shop, which was renowned locally for its delicious pastries. (*Ken Gravett/English Heritage*)

Nos 2, 4 and 6 New Rents, looking towards Forge Lane, September 1962. (*Ken Gravett/English Heritage*)

Hempsted Street, September 1962. For many, this was one of the most fascinating streets in the town. With its quaint terraces and wealth of architectural gems, it was a sad day for those born and raised there when it and the surrounding area were compulsorily purchased at the start of the 1960s. This view from Godinton Road shows the even-numbered terraced houses looking towards New Rents; these houses were destroyed just under two years later. (*Ken Gravett/English Heritage*)

Nos 6–16 Hempsted Street, looking from New Rents towards Godinton Road, September 1962. (*Ken Gravett/English Heritage*)

Hempsted Street, September 1962. One of the two premises in Hempsted Street that belonged to Danns furniture dealers can be seen here, sandwiched between no. 1 and no. 3a. Their other premises were opposite. No. 3a is already derelict. (*Ken Gravett/ English Heritage*)

Hempsted Street, seen from New Rents, September 1962. Danns furniture dealers can be seen on the left, together with nos 3a–11, which have already been boarded up to await their fate. (*Ken Gravett/English Heritage*)

Hempsted Street, looking towards New Rents and the Castle Hotel, September 1962. These old houses (nos 5–11) were already boarded up, awaiting demolition, even then. Note the old Nestlé's Milk advertisement just visible on the side wall. (*Ken Gravett/English Heritage*)

MEMORIES ARE MADE OF THESE 77

Hempsted Street, looking towards the Wellington Hotel, September 1962. The quaint frontages of nos 23–31 can be clearly seen. The former Wesleyan Church and Quaker meeting-house is on the immediate left, and was for many years used for furniture storage by W.H. Gibbs, until its demolition. (*Ken Gravett/English Heritage*)

Hempsted Street, September 1962. Even the lovely old cottages that stood at the junction of Tufton Street were not saved. Probably built in the Georgian era, nos 23–31 were architectural gems, and although they were already in a state of disrepair, their demolition created much sadness in the community. (*Ken Gravett/English Heritage*)

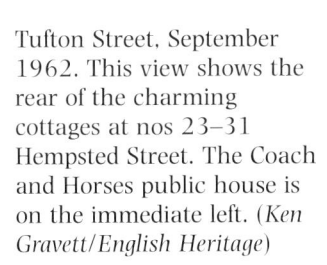

Tufton Street, September 1962. This view shows the rear of the charming cottages at nos 23–31 Hempsted Street. The Coach and Horses public house is on the immediate left. (*Ken Gravett/English Heritage*)

Hempsted Street, from the junction of Tufton Street and Regents Place and looking towards Godinton Road, August 1963. The quaint terraced houses at nos 32–72 can be seen on the right. The reputable business of Reg Paine, boot and shoe retailer and repairer, can be seen further down on the left (adjacent to the sun blind) at nos 41–43. (*Ken Gravett/English Heritage*)

Hempsted Street, September 1962. Even before this area was earmarked for redevelopment, a percentage of the properties in the street were derelict and in some cases had been for a number of years, as evidenced by the boarded-up windows and cracked plaster of nos 50–52. This was probably quite an attractive building at one time. (*Ken Gravett/English Heritage*)

Hempsted Street, August 1963. One of the town's many lost inns, the Coach and Horses at no. 26, stood on the corner of Hempsted Street and Regents Place opposite the Wellington Hotel, which was on the corner of Hempsted Street and Tufton Street. Just under ten years later these familiar haunts were no more. (*Ken Gravett/English Heritage*)

Hempsted Street, looking back towards New Rents, August 1963. Just three years later demolition started. (*Ken Gravett/ English Heritage*)

Hempsted Street, August 1963. The shanty-town appearance of Hempsted Street is seen here at its best – or its worst. (*Ken Gravett/ English Heritage*)

Hempsted Street, August 1963. G.A. Lee, turf accountant, now occupies the former premises of George Baker, furniture dealer. (*Ken Gravett/English Heritage*)

Hempsted Street, August 1963. A view of nos 8–12, on the other side of the road. The service entrance to the rear of the High Street premises can be seen on the immediate right. (*Ken Gravett/English Heritage*)

Hempsted Street, September 1962. Back in the 1960s, these architectural gems were regarded as worn out and worthy only of disposal. The case couldn't be more different today, as they would be much preferred to the architectural wilderness that replaced them. (*Ken Gravett/English Heritage*)

Hempsted Street, looking towards New Rents, September 1962. The building in the distance on the left-hand corner of Hempsted Street was for many years the premises of Nicholas Kingsman, bakers and confectioners, at 1–5 New Rents. Keen cyclists in the area will also remember W.M. Marshall, cycles and electrical retailer, at no. 4, also on the left. (*Ken Gravett/English Heritage*)

New Street, looking towards Maidstone Road, September 1962. The Roman Catholic church of St Teresa of Avila is on the extreme left in this view of nos 90–114. (*Ken Gravett/English Heritage*)

New Street, September 1962. These ancient cottages at nos 90–114 were demolished in 1973, together with the houses and business premises opposite, to create a new roundabout. The junction of Magazine Road is on the left, with the town centre in the distance on the right. (*Ken Gravett/English Heritage*)

New Street, September 1962. The Prince of Orange public house (also known as the 'Three Ones', being at 111 New Street), was for many years a popular stop-off for people travelling to and from the town on the main A20. These superb views show the popular hostelry when in the ownership of Courage and Barclay. The Prince of Orange became an Irish hostelry by the name of O'Brien's in the 1990s and more recently the building was knocked through to the neighbouring derelict Prince Albert, and it is now wholly the Prince Albert. The entrance to Barrow Hill and Engineers Court can be seen on the right of both pictures. (*Ken Gravett/English Heritage*)

Magazine Road, September 1962. This view shows the rear gardens of nos 90–114 New Street. (*Ken Gravett/English Heritage*)

Magazine Road, looking towards Canterbury Road, September 1962. Nos 2 and 4 were replaced by a roundabout in 1974. The well-known business premises of E.K. Chittenden, builder, contractor and joiner, can be seen beyond the car on the left. (*Ken Gravett/English Heritage*)

Magazine Road, looking towards New Street, September 1962. This is another view of the old cottages at nos 2 and 4. (*Ken Gravett/English Heritage*)

Magazine Road, September 1962. This view shows the derelict cottages at nos 8–12, adjacent to the rear access to properties in Kent Avenue, Hayward's Garage and Snashall's Bakery. Another of the old-style road signs is on the right. (*Ken Gravett/English Heritage*)

Tufton Street, September 1962. For many years funeral director F.C. Wood has traded from premises at 21 Tufton Street. Here the familiar building can be seen sandwiched between Stanhay (Ashford) Ltd, garage and workshops, at no. 23, and the popular Swan Hotel, where the licensee at the time was L.F. Bridgewater. (*Ken Gravett/English Heritage*)

Tufton Street, September 1962. Another part of Ashford that isn't instantly recognisable, although the church spires may assist. For a number of years J.W. Hall's played a large part in the lives of those do-it-yourself enthusiasts of the 1960s. As ironmongers and builders merchants, they occupied a large section of the street at nos 1–13. (*Ken Gravett/English Heritage*)

4
Everlasting Nostalgia

Chambers Garage, North Street, 1957. Chambers Garage, at the corner of Ringway and North Street, is seen here in pre-Ringway days, when reputable businessman Leo Chambers owned the business. In the early days Leo started his business in Park Street, behind the old *Kentish Express* offices in the High Street. In 1957 you could buy two brands of fuel from the same forecourt, which is impossible nowadays. Notice the old lorry of C.I. Epps the builders in the background. (*Terry Woodcock*)

Chambers Garage, North Street, 1957. Another view of the garage, with two mechanics standing inside the entrance to the workshop. The building with the chimney stack in the background still survives. The garage site is completely unrecognisable today. Blue Line Lane (which today runs through the site) can be seen on the left. (*Terry Woodcock*)

Chambers Garage, North Street, *c.* 1968. In late 1968 kindly gentleman Ken Woodcock purchased the business, retaining the Chambers name. Ken is seen here on the garage forecourt with a gleaming Morris 1000 convertible, looking rather pleased with himself. (*Terry Woodcock*)

Chambers Garage, North Street, c. 1969. Ken, seen here outside the tiny workshops, certainly enjoyed his work. (*Terry Woodcock*)

North Street, 1970. Such pumps were a familiar sight around the country at this time. The Shell globes on top of the pumps used to light up at night. Today the globes themselves are collectors' items and are much sought after. The house in the background was demolished in the 1980s and replaced with individual flats. (*Terry Woodcock*)

North Street, 1972. The old-style pumps have disappeared during the alterations to the garage, but business seems to be continuing regardless. (*Terry Woodcock*)

North Street, 1973. A busy day at the garage, with parked cars probably waiting for MOTs or servicing. (*Terry Woodcock*)

North Street, 1973. This dramatic view was taken during the construction of the Ringway – hence the houses being demolished on the right. Lavender's Bed and Breakfast is in the background. (*Terry Woodcock*)

North Street, 1973. This must be one of the last views of the Somerset Arms public house before its demolition, here showing the newly installed canopy over the garage. The construction of Charter House is under way in the background (top right). (*Terry Woodcock*)

North Street, 1973. The alterations are nearing completion, and the canopy is being given a lick of paint in the familiar Shell colours – red, white and yellow. (*Terry Woodcock*)

North Street, 1973. You wouldn't see a lady dressed like this filling up with fuel today! How fashion tastes have changed over the years. (*Terry Woodcock*)

North Street from Charter House, 1973. In pre-Ringway days, Chambers Garage was located along North Street, but after the completion of the infamous scheme, it gained in many respects as a slip road to the garage from the Ringway was included in the plans. (*Terry Woodcock*)

North Street, 1980. This memorable view of the garage site was taken shortly before major alterations were to take place, which included new workshops and a 'Shell Shop'. (*Terry Woodcock*)

North Street, 1985. Two years after the major alterations, Chambers Garage is seen here from the roof of the Edinburgh Road car park. Further alterations have since taken place, including updated forecourt facilities and a new shop. Ken's son Terry continues to excel in business here under the name of Andrews at Chambers. He is also locally known for his 'all-year-round' Christmas decorations on the roof of the workshops, which he never takes down! (*Terry Woodcock*)

This aerial view from 1970 shows the popular landmark of East Hill Mill (Pledges Mill). Most of the mill was destroyed in the fire in 1974; the houses on the left at the rear of the mill complex have since been demolished too. (*Bob and Jean Turner*)

East Hill, 1964. The beautiful old cottages of A. & W. Mummery, nurserymen, were demolished shortly after this picture was taken to provide space for a new all-weather netball court and latterly a car park. (*Bob and Jean Turner*)

High Street (lower), 1969. The last days of nos 15, 17a and 17b. Demolition was about to start, to judge by the signs and wooden battens across the shop fronts. They were replaced by two-storey retail and office premises. Note the ornate gable end on the upper elevation of nos 17a and 17b. (*Bob and Jean Turner*)

Hempsted Street, 1965. These once cherished and charming cottages, 32–48 Hempsted Street, are seen here during the early days of demolition. (*Mr J. Jackman/Alan Ward*)

Hempsted Street, 1965. Another view showing nos 32–48 under demolition. The Coach and Horses public house can be seen in the background. (*Mr J. Jackman/Alan Ward*)

High Street (lower), *c.* 1952. The former premises of Stevenson's fishmonger and greengrocer at 45–49 High Street are under demolition. The high-class grocer G.V. Crump's can be seen on the left, with Scott's dyers and cleaners on the right. The new building that replaced the original nos 45–49 was for many years occupied by Kennington Laundry, Baldwins Travel Service and Tudor Rose, drapers, respectively. (*Reflections/Weavers*)

An accident in Queen Street, at the junction with Bank Street, 1962. In the absence of emergency services, local passers-by stand ready to assist. It is understood that the driver of the vehicle was not seriously injured and walked away from the crash unaided. The Corn Exchange is on the immediate left. (*Reflections/Weavers*)

A late winter's evening in High Street (middle), 1952. The view is looking towards the upper High Street and the Castle Hotel, and Worger's and Achille Serre can be seen on the left. This is one of the many classic images taken by the late Weaver Brothers. (*Reflections/Weavers*)

High Street (lower), 1967. Here is a fascinating window display from Headley's grocers at 46 High Street. A staff member stands proudly outside holding a certificate and a trophy, no doubt for a product that they were successfully promoting at the time. This store closed in 1976 after larger chains began to force smaller shops out of business. (*Mrs Lednor*)

High Street (lower), 1967. This superb window display at Headley's was one of many over the years that attracted the eye of the Ashford housewife. In this 1967 view there are tinned pears for *2s 1d*, orange squash for *3s 11d*, Lyle's golden syrup for *2s 8d* and Golden Shred marmalade for *4s 3d*. The display was entitled 'Golden Fare for Golden Days'. (*Mrs Lednor*)

Bank Street, December 1975. On a miserable and wet day, here we see the Royal Insurance Offices at no. 17. Next door the Trustee Savings Bank occupied no. 19 before moving further down Bank Street to the former premises of Douglas Weaver's camera shop and the Ashford Co-operative Dry Cleaners at nos 29 and 29a. The vacant premises beyond, no. 21, were formerly shared by Freeman, Hardy & Willis, boot and shoe retailers, and Foster Finn-Kelcey, chartered accountants. (S&K)

Bank Street, c. 1975. Many style-conscious Ashford gentlemen will remember the popular menswear business of G. Edbrooke, whose premises at no. 15 were previously occupied by G. Herbert and Co. Ltd, pawnbrokers, jewellers, outfitters and furniture dealers. For many years previously Edbrooke's had occupied 31 High Street, now the Halifax estate agents. (S&K)

High Street (middle), 1977. In the years before the construction of Phase two of the Tufton shopping centre, Marks & Spencer occupied nos 64–66. Their High Street premises are seen here shortly before the company moved to brand-new premises at the top of the High Street. The building was later split and remodelled to become Barclays Bank adjacent to the George Hotel and Cordon Bleu frozen foods to the right, adjacent to Timothy Whites. (*S&K*)

High Street (lower), 1976. Pearl Assurance House (now Northdown House) was built to replace those premises knocked down at the junction of High Street and Station Road (*see* Chapter 1). At no. 1 Hallam Interiors, selling china, carpets and glassware, dominated the site until the late 1970s, when Bassett's Furnishings took over the extensive retail premises. More recently Pizza Hut acquired the building for their popular town centre restaurant. (*S&K*)

Right: High Street (lower), 1962. The fabulous 1960s-style interior of Gizzi's Restaurant at 29 High Street is seen here shortly after Antonio and Vilma Gizzi opened for business. Nowadays the restaurant is called Café Express but it's still very popular. Proprietor Ufuk Chen vows that he will never change the retro design, which surprisingly looks much the same forty-four years later.

Below left: High Street (lower), 1962. An early view of the upper floor of Gizzi's. In 1962 this design was ahead of its time. The stained-glass window painting still survives today, although it is somewhat faded.

Below right: High Street (lower), 1962. Menu-laden tables on the upper floor of Gizzi's.

Queen Street, at its junction with Church Road, looking towards Bank Street, 1962. The wall and building on the right were demolished in 1964 to make way for the new Ashford Library, which opened in 1966. (*Bryan Sales*)

Elwick Road, 1962. This is another nostalgic view taken by the late Bryan Sales, who worked for Ashford Urban District Council. Part of his job was to photograph and survey the town's streets. Traffic flow and new developments were his forte. Elwick Road is seen here at a time when traffic was still two-way. Eastes and Loud corn merchants' warehouse (more recently N.V. nightclub) can be seen in the background. Note the old *Kentish Express* van on the left, with its personalised registration plate 'KE4'. (*Bryan Sales*)

New Street, 1967. Caffyn's Ltd in New Street was another of the reputable garages in Ashford for many years, having taken over from Charles Hayward, which had previously occupied the site for over seventy-five years. At this site Caffyn's sold Austin, Triumph and Rover cars over the years, before moving to Henwood in 1988. The familiar premises illustrated here were demolished in 1989.

New Street, 1967. Just across the road from their showroom was Caffyn's filling station, which was situated in one corner of the Gravel Walk car park. The site was acquired in 1986 by Safeway Supermarkets Ltd, and a new supermarket opened there shortly afterwards. Caffyn's still trade in Ashford at the Orbital Business Park, dealing in Vauxhall and Skoda cars.

Maidstone Road, November 1968. It wasn't until 1973 that this accident black spot was altered. This picture shows traffic venturing out of the infamous Chart Road/Western Avenue junction before the alterations, which included the blocking of Western Avenue, a new roundabout in Magazine Road and Maidstone Road being made a dual carriageway from Highworth School towards the bypass. Traffic was therefore made one-way on this stretch outside Furley Hall and the former St Teresa Roman Catholic School. (*Ashford Borough Council*)

The old Royal Mail sorting office on the corner of Elwick Road and Station Road, 1969. The premises illustrated here were situated on land next to the former South Kent College campus. In 1976 this sorting office was demolished for the widening of Station Road, and the Royal Mail temporarily used the old Drill Hall in Newtown Road (now demolished) until 1986, when a new purpose-built office was constructed on the former Ministry of Pensions site at the corner of Tannery Lane and Station Road. (*Mr Jackman/Alan Ward*)

Gridlock in Station Road during the widening works, 1978. The old sorting office has already gone and the College refectory and main buildings can be seen on the right. The Kent Arms public house is in the distance on the left, adjacent to Ashford domestic station. (*Ashford Borough Council*)

Traffic is queuing towards Beaver Road during the widening works in Station Road, 1978. The cast-iron gates are all that's left of the former sorting office on the left. The former Ashford Library can be seen (below the trees), as well as Kent House, Ashford Working Men's Club, Crouches Garage and the Kent Arms public house on the right. Note the prices of four star and two star petrol back in 1978, just adjacent to the lady who obviously enjoyed being photographed. (*Ashford Borough Council*)

Station Road, 1978. Further along Station Road, where it joins the railway bridge, police guide an articulated lorry laden with an enormous mechanical earth-mover. The Butchers Hotel can be seen in the distance. (*Ashford Borough Council*)

Station Road, 1978. The huge heavy goods vehicle manoeuvres into position, with an old Rover SD1 police car calming the traffic behind. The contractors for the works were Dowsett, who also constructed much of the Ashford–Folkestone stretch of the M20. (*Ashford Borough Council*)

Station Road, 1978. Off-loading the Caterpillar earth-mover, with the Rover SD1 police car to the left. Flared trousers and longer hair were still the trend in 1978, as illustrated by the bystanders. (*Ashford Borough Council*)

Elwick Road, 1978. Builders' materials from the alteration works litter the frontage of South Kent College. Elwick Road had earlier been widened back in 1971, and this view shows the group of trees that once stood where the Laing O'Rourke construction offices currently stand. Many will also remember Elwick Gardens, nurserymen and florists, and the former AUDC slipper baths which once stood along this stretch of Elwick Road. (*Ashford Borough Council*)

Elwick Road, at the junction with Church Road, 1978. It was only in 2005 that this notorious junction was reopened to through traffic, having been closed since 1983. While Station Road was being widened, police traffic control was required on the junction. (*Ashford Borough Council*)

The new roundabout in Station Road, 1978. The works are nearing completion. South Kent College and the former Social Services offices can be seen on the left. (*Ashford Borough Council*)

Station Road, 1978. This view of the new roundabout also shows the flour mills of H.S. Pledge in Victoria Road. Almost six years after this picture was taken, and ten years after a similar incident at their former East Hill premises, a disastrous fire destroyed this familiar landmark in September 1984, resulting in the complete demolition of the mill that was built originally in 1890. (*Ashford Borough Council*)

Edinburgh Road, 1980. At this time these derelict buildings and former residential dwellings were owned by Charter Consolidated, and were the few properties still remaining on the adjacent site. The site itself, comprising Park Street, Wolseley Road, Park Road and Stone Street, had been earmarked for redevelopment, but the site was largely derelict and was a playground for vandals. The council urged Charter to clean up these eyesores and the surrounding land, and in 1985 work started on a new shopping centre, which eventually opened in 1987 as Park Mall.

Edinburgh Road, 1981. Following the council's plea, the derelict dwellings seen here were gradually dismantled, some of them having stood in this state since the late 1970s. The white-fronted property on the left was at one time occupied by well-known Ashford chiropodist Philip G. Dormer.

Victoria Mills, Victoria Road, September 1984. Scores of firemen attended the blaze from stations far and wide, and the main railway line (in the foreground) had to be closed. Their other premises at East Hill had also been largely destroyed in similar circumstances, and the police blamed arsonists for this blaze. The shell of the once-thriving 1890 flour mill, all that remained after the fire, was demolished in the months following the disaster.

Victoria Mills, September 1984, photographed from the railway bridge. The fierce flames are licking away at the tinder dry mill as fire crews struggle to get the blaze under control. It burned throughout the night.

Kent House, Station Road, 1965. This view shows the early days of Kent House when C.L. and H.L. Blundell occupied the ground floor. Charter Consolidated occupied the upper floors at this time, before the construction of their office complex in Park Street. The Employment Service and Black Horse finance now occupy the ground floor, while Eurostar (UK) Ltd largely occupies the upper floors.

Chart Road, 1964. Many will remember the prominent premises of AID Garages Ltd on the corner of Chart Road and Godinton Road, which at the time were Standard and Triumph dealers. This fascinating view shows the popular garage in its heyday. Thousands of Ashfordians purchased their cars or fuel here until it closed in 1994 while trading as a Fiat and Skoda dealership known as Ashford Motor Company. The garage and surrounding warehouse units were subsequently demolished for the new Channel Tunnel High Speed rail link. (*Reflections/Weavers 1964/6171*)

Side view of the AID Garage in Chart Road, 1964. The garage also offered Mobil and Singer Service. Note the absence of a canopy over the forecourt. (*Reflections/Weavers 1964/6172*)

The garage workshops in Godinton Road, 1964. (*Reflections/Weavers 1964/6173*)

Tufton Centre, 1975. This is Ashford's first Tesco Home 'n' Wear store on its opening day. When the store closed on 1 August 1987, locals were left with competitor Sainsbury's store to shop at in the town centre. Littlewoods (now BHS) moved into the former supermarket premises, and later Tesco opened a new store at the former Crooksfoot site in Hythe Road. They did at the time though have a somewhat dated store at Brookfield Road that they bought from local business entrepreneur Lew Cartier (now Matalan). (*www.tescopix.com*)

Cartier's Freezer Foods at the corner of Brookfield and Chart Roads, 1976. Owner Lew Cartier, who also had stores in Faversham, sold everything from the obvious to wine and spirits, clothes and general grocery products. Many will remember the branded Peter Dominic wine shop that was set into an alcove on the trading floor. Mr Cartier also had premises at Mace Lane industrial estate at one time.

The wine shop in Cartier's store, Brookfield Road, December 1976. Many of the alcoholic beverages of the past can be seen here, including Watney's Party Seven, Watney's Crown and Watney's Export. You could purchase a bottle of Martini Rosso for £1.29 and a four-pack of Watney's Export for 55p. How times have changed.

Ashford School, c. 1950. Ashford School was founded in 1898 by Mrs Thimann, wife of the Revd I.P. Thimann, minister of the Congregational Church, who opened a small school in Queens Road, Ashford. After moving to a succession of sites in the town, the school found premises in East Hill in 1913, where it remains to this day. Here are some of the original buildings on the site: (left to right) Alfred, Somerville and Coronation Houses. Over the years the school has expanded and gone from strength to strength. (*Lambert Weston*)

The unforgettable Miss Lillian Brake at her retirement from Ashford School, 1955. For over forty years, she gave her all to the school, latterly as principal, and played a key role in making the school what it is today. In 1952 she received an OBE for her services to education, and she was much loved and respected by generations of staff and pupils of the school. She sadly died in 1960 at the age of 76 after a short illness, just five years into her retirement. (*Ashford School*)

High Street (lower), 1953. Miss Brake and the Archbishop of Canterbury leave the Odeon in the High Street after the 1953 school prize-giving ceremony. (*Reflections/Weavers*)

EVERLASTING NOSTALGIA 117

High Street (lower), 1954. It might look like an early example of the Riverdance, but this is how Miss Brake led her girls through the town safely. (*Reflections/Weavers 1954/3003*)

High Street (lower), 1954. Miss Brake awaits her girls, to teach them the correct way to cross the road – a practice familiar to generations of Ashford School girls. (*Reflections/Weavers 1954/3004*)

Council Chambers, Kings Parade, 5 May 1955. Miss Brake is seen here at one of her many presentations by Ashford Urban District Council. The gentleman wearing the chain of office is Mr H.L. Gibbs. (*Reflections/Weavers*)

Council Chambers, Kings Parade, 5 May 1955. Showing her gratitude, Miss Brake shakes hands with members of the Urban District Council after her presentation. (*Reflections/Weavers*)

High Street (lower), 1956. Another of the annual prize-giving ceremonies. From left to right: Miss Nightingale (who became principal on Miss Brake's retirement), Miss Baker, Lady Mountbatten, Professor Cullis, and behind them Lord and Lady Brabourne. Sadly Professor Cullis died twelve days after this photograph was taken. (*Reflections/Weavers 1956/3182*)

High Street (lower), 1959. The guests of honour, the Earl and Countess Mountbatten, leave the Odeon after the 1959 prize-giving ceremony with their daughter Lady Brabourne. (*Reflections/Weavers 1959/5543*)

High Street (lower), 1959. Locals wait to catch a glimpse of the departing Lord Mountbatten after the 1959 prize-giving. (*Reflections/Weavers 1959/5542*)

High Street (lower), 1962. The Rt Hon. William Deedes addressing the school at the 1962 prize-giving held at the Odeon. (*Reflections/Weavers*)

Ashford School, 1970. Lord Brabourne makes his speech at the prize-giving ceremony in the presence of his wife and Lady Prudence Loudon. (*Kent Messenger*)

High Street (lower), 1971. The much-loved Duchess of Kent talking to Ashfordians, while in town for another prize-giving at the Odeon. (*Kentish Express*)

High Street (lower), 1971. Miss Nightingale and the Duchess of Kent entering the Odeon for the annual prize-giving. Note the nervous-looking young lady in the Musketeer outfit in the centre. (*Kent Messenger*)

High Street (lower), 1971. The Duchess of Kent outside the Odeon, talking to Miss Nightingale, with Lady Prudence Loudon and Miss Churchill standing centre and right. (*Kent Messenger*)

Ashford School, 1971. Miss Smith is presented to the duchess, with Miss Baker in the foreground. (*Kent Messenger*)

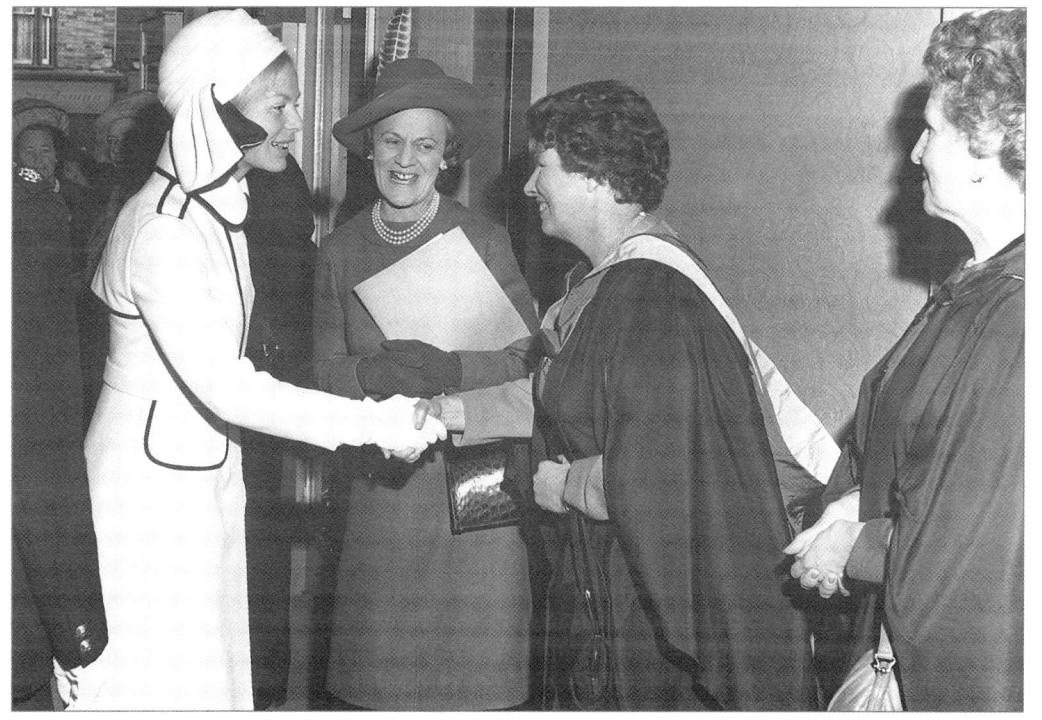

High Street (lower), 1971. The Duchess of Kent acknowledges Miss Nightingale. (*Kent Messenger*)

Ashford School, 1971. Pupils wave off the Duchess of Kent's royal car. As well as the prize-giving, she was at the school to open a new wing. (*Kent Messenger*)

The opening of Ashford School's new Festival Wing by Sir Hugh Knatchbull-Hugesson during the Open Day, 28 May 1952. (*Reflections/Weavers 1952/1409*)

Lady Brabourne laying the foundation stone of Jubilee Wing, 4 July 1959. (*Reflections/Weavers 1959/2539*)

Following Lady Brabourne's laying of the foundation stone the previous year, the Archbishop of Canterbury Dr Fisher opens Jubilee Wing on 27 May 1960. (*Kentish Express*)

Dr Fisher talks to the girls in the new Domestic Science room in Jubilee Wing, 27 May 1960. (*Kentish Express*)

HRH Princess Margaret is seen opening the Lillian Brake Building on 6 December 1966, in memory of the school's much-loved former principal, who died six years earlier. (*Kent Messenger*)

Another of the school's many building projects, the new junior common room, was opened by the Duchess of Kent on 3 November 1971. (*Kentish Express*)

Retired principal Miss Mary Nightingale, accompanied by Mr David Harrison of Harrison Clague Architects, lays the foundation stone for the new Alfred Wing, 28 March 1973.

5

Round & About

A rare view of Watercress Estate in 1962, showing the new houses built alongside Victoria Park. The grassed area on the left is where the high-rise flats now stand. The road illustrated here is today totally unrecognisable. (*Bryan Sales*)

The neighbouring Brookfield Estate, 7 May 1962. Construction is still in its early stages . . . (*Bryan Sales*)

. . . but just two months later, on 20 July, the Brookfield properties are nearing completion. (*Bryan Sales*)

Canterbury Road, Kennington, 1958. These properties still survive. They were originally built as fire brigade houses. They front on to Canterbury Road, and the fire station was situated behind them, before its demolition in 1997 when the fire service relocated. (*Kent Fire and Rescue Museum*)

Bybrook Road, Kennington, 1958. These houses at the bottom of Bybrook Road are clearly recognisable. (*Kent Fire and Rescue Museum*)

Bybrook Road, Kennington, 1958. Many of the houses that backed on to the fire station actually had their own 'emergency access' to the station, with a convenient pathway and gate to the site. The former station site is soon to become a new meeting house for the Church of Jesus Christ and the Latter Day Saints. (*Kent Fire and Rescue Museum*)

Bybrook Road, Kennington, 3 August 1965. The former burgermeister of Ashford's twin town Bad Munstereifel, Herr Theodor Heuel is seen here unveiling a plaque naming a new block of flats in Bybrook Road. Heuel House, named after the burgermeister, is one of five blocks bordering the road, and is situated at the top of Bybrook Road where it joins The Pasture. The plaque can still be seen today. (*Ashford Borough Council*)

Canterbury Road, 1965. Before the introduction of traffic lights, Penlee Point, at the fork of the A28 and A251, was another of the town's accident black spots. The road was much narrower than it is today, and it was extensively altered in the mid-1970s in a bid to make it safer, but it wasn't until the introduction of traffic lights that the accident rate decreased significantly. (*Jenny Marshall*)

Canterbury Road, Kennington, *c.* 1950. These wartime Nissen huts used to be situated near the site of the current Hayesbank Surgery in Cemetery Lane and the Canterbury Road motorway bridge. Kent Fire Brigade used them as their district fire station after leaving Kings Parade and before their new station was opened at Bybrook in the late 1950s. (*Kent Fire and Rescue Museum*)

Church Road, Kennington, c. 1965. This rare view shows one of three Crouch's premises in the town over the years. This one in Church Road and another in Hythe Road are the only two left trading today. Their third, in Station Road, together with its Ford dealership, closed in 1992 after trading on the site for over forty years. The derelict former premises were demolished in February and March 2006. (*Jenny Marshall*)

Canterbury Road, Kennington, 1975. The Croft Hotel, at the junction of Canterbury Road and The Street, is seen here before its expansion in the 1980s. This popular hotel, which is still trading today, is one of three along this stretch of the A28, the other two being the Conningbrook (previously known as the Pilgrims Rest, the Master Spearpoint and Spearpoint Hotel) and the Holiday Inn (previously Forte Posthouse and Trusthouse Forte Post House). (*Jenny Marshall*)

Canterbury Road, 1975. The popular Golden Ball hostelry has for many years attracted a regular clientele in its position on the A28 at the junction of Ball Lane. The former coaching inn was in the past known for its bat and trap tournaments and it has an extensive and very pleasant beer garden attached. The former mill where Henry Sturges Pledge started his business is situated at the rear of the site. (*Jenny Marshall*)

Canterbury Road, 1971. Many Kennington youngsters of the past will remember the premises of Harry Osband, newsagent and tobacconist. The quaint tin-roofed premises at no. 403 were not dissimilar to Arkwright's shop in BBC Television's *Open All Hours*. One Kennington resident commented that Mr Osband used to serve him with his grandfather's pipe tobacco at the age of 7. He went on to say that Mr Osband stood very upright, had a wide leather belt and used to grunt rather than speak while serving. It is now a residential property, and the old shop premises have been converted into an extension to the house. (*Jenny Marshall*)

The Street, Kennington, 1978. These premises at the top of The Street in Kennington have for many years been occupied by a number of businesses in the construction trade, notably J. & R. Raven Builders and more recently Sandells Maintenance Ltd. Ravenscourt Plant & Hire occupy the premises in this view. (*Jenny Marshall*)

The Rose, Faversham Road, Kennington, 1966. This well-known watering hole at the junction of Faversham Road and Ulley Road has seen many changes over the years, and recently received an internal makeover, including a new public bar. (*Jenny Marshall*)

The old Bybrook Tavern, Canterbury Road, Kennington, 1970. Seen here in its Courage and Barclay days, this hostelry was always popular with local people and those en route to Canterbury. The original Bybrook Tavern closed in 1982 and a year later Trusthouse Forte purchased it and extended the premises to become the Post House Hotel. More recently, after the Forte group had been purchased, the Post House became a Holiday Inn. (*Jenny Marshall*)

The Spearpoint Hotel, Spearpoint Corner, Kennington, 1975. This hotel has seen many alterations, including several name changes. Latterly known as the Master Spearpoint, this classy hotel was purchased by Fullers and extensively refurbished and extended to become the Pilgrims Rest in 1999. A further change came in 2005, together with a new name, when Shepherd Neame took it over and it was officially renamed the Conningbrook by the late Gordon Turner, former Mayor, councillor and authority on the history of the area. (*Jim Ashby*)

The Towers Secondary School, Faversham Road, Kennington, 1975. The school opened in 1967 and has undergone many changes over the years. It is currently on its fourth headmaster, Malcolm Ramsay, who took over in 2000. Previous headmasters were Geoffrey Foster (1967–85), Paul Howson (1986–9) and Adrian Brown (1990–9). As well as changes in headship, the school has been progressively extended in recent years.

The church of St Mary the Virgin, Ball Lane, Kennington, 1961. The carefully tended allotments (which are no more) give the church with its Norman tower a far better outlook and appearance than it enjoys today. (*Jim Ashby*)

School Field, Bybrook Road, Kennington, 1964. This is Bybrook County Infants School soon after its completion. Today the school is known as Phoenix Community School but it is destined for demolition in early 2007 when a new school is built on the former Junior School site. (*Jenny Marshall*)

Great Chart School, 1964. Before their days at both Bybrook schools, Donald and Margaret Samuel were based at Great Chart School where Donald was headmaster. This charming view shows the devoted couple with some youngsters outside one of the prefabricated classrooms. The school became a private house when new premises were built in Singleton. It was thanks to their devotion to their pupils that Donald was offered the headship at Bybrook a few months later. (*D.U. Samuel*)

Bybrook Infants School, Kennington, 1964. This classroom classic shows Donald in his early days at Bybrook Infants. Donald chose the name for the two sites after the original name – Ashford Kennington South Junior Mixed and Infants (JMI) Primary School – was deemed too wordy. Note the houses in Bybrook Road under construction in the background. (*D.U. Samuel*)

Bybrook Infants School, 1969. When the Samuels came to Bybrook in 1965 there were just 67 pupils. Here is Margaret Samuel (left) with Class 1 in 1969. When I attended Bybrook between 1979 and 1983, the classes were not numbered; instead they had names such as Kites, Pebbles and so on. (*D.U. Samuel*)

Bybrook Infants School, 1977. By this time Donald and Margaret had been at the junior school for seven years. Donald was succeeded as the Infants School head by Vanessa Seal, and this view shows the Queen's Silver Jubilee celebrations in the playground.

The official opening of Bybrook Junior School, 1970. From left to right: Donald Samuel (Headmaster), John Haynes (County Education Officer), the Revd E.B. Lewis (Vicar of Kennington), Bill Shrubsole (Divisional Education Officer) and Cllr Wilfred Gower (Chairman of Ashford Urban District Council). (*D.U. Samuel*)

Bybrook Junior School, Kennington, 1970. Donald and Margaret Samuel take turns to be photographed with Class 3 of 1970. (*D.U. Samuel*)

Bybrook Junior School, 1970. Rows of children gather for the first assembly on opening day. Two teachers look on in the background, with Margaret Samuel in the centre. (*D.U. Samuel*)

Bybrook Junior School, 3 June 1970. How many Ashfordians can spot themselves in this official group photograph from June 1970? Margaret Samuel is on the right of the gathering. (*D.U. Samuel*)

Bybrook Junior School, c. 1973. Back row, left to right: Valerie Licence, Mrs Boardman, -?-, Mr Thorgerson, -?-. Front row: -?-, Miss Jones (Deputy Head), Donald Samuel (Head), Margaret Samuel, -?-, -?-. (*D.U. Samuel*)

Margaret Samuel in action at Bybrook Junior School, c. 1978. (*D.U. Samuel*)

Bybrook Junior School, 1977. It's the staff's turn to play the fool on this fun day, at which many of the male teachers are dressed as women. The gentleman (centre) with a no. 1 on his bike and wearing a tee-shirt saying 'Virginia Wade' may have been a fan as Virginia won Wimbledon in that year. (*D.U. Samuel*)

Hythe Road, Willesborough, 1967. This beautiful house once stood on the site of the current Tesco Extra at Willesborough. In its early days Crooksfoot had been an exclusive property, but by this time it had been separated into several dwellings. It will always be remembered for its stylish green-tiled roof and substantial surrounding acres of land. (*S&K*)

Hythe Road, Willesborough, 1988. These two sad pictures show Crooksfoot in its derelict state. In 1983 its land was used for site offices while the new M20 between Ashford and Folkestone was being constructed. The house itself was demolished shortly after these pictures were taken when work commenced on the new supermarket. (*Alan Ward*)

The notorious Willesborough Interchange at Junction 10 of the M20 under construction, 1981. The interchange, which opened together with the motorway seen below in 1983, is renowned for traffic jams, gridlock and numerous sets of traffic lights. Work is due to begin to improve the roundabout in late 2006. (*Peter Goodwin*)

Open day at Willesborough Interchange, Junction 10, 1983. Such open days are common practice in the United Kingdom when new motorways open. A similar open day was held on the Ashford– Maidstone stretch in May 1991. (*Peter Goodwin*)

The M20, Willesborough, 1983. These two memorable views illustrate the conversion of the old bypass into the M20 and the realignment of Hythe Road. (*Peter Goodwin*)

A fair at Newtown Green, 1952. Many fairs were held on the green over the decades.

This superb aerial view shows the extensive site of the Ashford North County Secondary School for Boys in Essella Road in 1967. Nowadays the school is mixed and is known as the North School. It is currently undergoing a huge refurbishment and rebuilding programme. When some of the old classrooms were knocked down, old wartime bunkers were found beneath them. Essella Road and the old Ashford Football Ground can be seen at the top. (*Simmons Aerofilms*)

The Norton Knatchbull Grammar School in 1967, when it was still very much underdeveloped. Hythe Road runs from top to bottom on the left, and the railway line to Canterbury passes along the foreground. The old school buildings that fronted Hythe Road were demolished in the 1990s and the site has recently become home to a brand-new nursing home. Like the North School, the Norton School is also currently undergoing substantial construction works. (*Simmons Aerofilms*)

In 1988 serious floods inundated the marshy areas adjacent to the town centre. The Southern orbital road has not yet been built but Ellingham industrial estate is at centre left. Before the construction of Asda, B&Q and the Designer Outlet Village, locals spoke of their concerns about building on this flood plain, so much of the construction was completed using stilts to raise the foundations of the premises concerned. (*FotoFlite*)

Park Farm, Kingsnorth, 1988, shortly before its demolition. Many newcomers to the town will not know that this charming house gave the comprehensive Park Farm housing estate its name. (*Alan Ward*)

6

Haven't We Been Here Before?

The Tufton Centre under construction on the former residential streets of Hempsted Street, Middle Street and Tufton Street, 1974. This view is looking towards Godinton Road, with the rear of the head post office in Tufton Street on the left. Apsley Street is adjacent to the smaller crane on the right. The Centre Square of the shopping complex (now known as County Square) is positioned roughly where the site offices are (below the larger crane). (*Reflections/Weavers 1974/0303*)

The main concrete and steelwork installations on the Tufton Centre site, 1974. This view is looking towards Godinton Road and Bank Street, and the Methodist Church can be seen on the left. (*Reflections/Weavers 1974/0578*)

The main support work is already taking shape in this photograph, taken at the Godinton Road/South Mall end of the centre in 1974. (*Reflections/Weavers 1974/1117*)

The Tufton Centre was Ashford's first major shopping centre, and it is seen here in the early months of its construction in 1974. The Godinton Road stretch of the Ringway is at the bottom, with Bank Street leading into the High Street on the right. Caffyn's Garage and New Street, together with an unfinished section of the Ringway, can also be seen at centre right. (*Reflections/Weavers 1974/1524*)

This closer view, taken a few months after as the picture above, shows West Street, Norwood Gardens, Forge Lane, Regents Place and the Telephone Exchange on the left. The church of St Mary the Virgin and the police station can be seen at top right. (*Reflections/Weavers 1974/1525*)

This unusual view of the Tufton Centre is looking towards South Ashford. North Street, Edinburgh Road, Wolseley Road and Park Road can all be seen at the bottom. Bank Street is to the left of the Tufton Centre in the middle, with the High Street running parallel to the church from left to right. (*Reflections/Weavers 1974/1527*)

The Tufton Centre is taking shape in this view of the South Square. Tufton Street runs parallel with the workman on the left. The giant Charter House complex is nearing completion in the distance. (*Reflections/Weavers 1974/1939*)

Another excellent aerial view from 1974 showing the swift progress of the shopping centre construction. Today's site, the County Square Extension, can be clearly seen in a wedge shape between the rear of the centre at Godinton Road and the Ringway. (*Reflections/Weavers 1974/1521*)

Just under a month later the roof has started to be laid, and the construction work is gradually winding down. (*Reflections/Weavers 1974/1754*)

The Tufton Centre, 1975. This is the service area to the rear of lower Bank Street and Middle Street. During the preliminary works to the current extension, an argument has broken out regarding delivery access via the unadopted road that is seen here running behind the Methodist Church towards Godinton Road. Doubtless traders faced the same problem in 1975. (*Reflections/ Weavers 1975/0053*)

The Tufton Centre in 1975, during the last weeks of construction. Bank Street is in the centre, with the police station at bottom right. At top right is the junction between the High Street, New Rents and Castle Street. (*Reflections/Weavers 1975/0598*)

This splendid 1976 view shows the finished Tufton Centre and the newly completed Ringway at the bottom. Phase two of the Tufton development had not yet begun as Lewis & Hyland's New Rents premises can still be seen dominating the top of the town. (*Reflections/Weavers 1976/0694*)

The Tufton Centre in 1983, ten years after work originally started. The derelict former Stanhay site to the rear is currently the subject of the new County Square extension, which has been on the cards since 1973. (*Ashford Borough Council*)

This and the following pictures all show the County Square Extension in 2006. Thirty-three years after work on the original shopping centre began, the tarmac is being removed from the former Stanhay car park and the adjacent stretch of Godinton Road, which will be buried underneath the new extension. (*Steve Salter*)

This is Godinton Road at its junction with Bank Street. Through traffic had already been diverted when this picture was taken, but pedestrians were allowed for a few more weeks. Popular take-away Kent Kebabs is on the right. (*Steve Salter*)

This sentimental view shows Godinton Road at its junction with the last remaining part of Hempsted Street, shortly before it disappeared forever. Trafalgar House is in the background. (*Steve Salter*)

The County Square Extension, looking towards Bank Street and Queen Street. Nick Francis (nearest the road) is Laing O'Rourke's site manager for the project. (*Steve Salter*)

The ever-popular Oranges Café Bar, on the corner of Apsley Street, is still very much in business despite the construction works. (*Steve Salter*)

Here provision is being made for traffic signage and islands, to divert vehicles wishing to use the County Square car park along Apsley Street, where a temporary entrance has been made. (*Steve Salter*)

The temporary pedestrian access from Apsley Street to Bank Street, shortly before its closure. (*Steve Salter*)

This bird's-eye view, taken by professional photographer Ian Gambrill, shows the ongoing works and the full extent of the County Square Extension site. (*Reflections/Weavers 2006/5789*)

Acknowledgements

Over the years many local people and companies have been extremely kind and patient in assisting me with my research. Many have given me very valuable information, which has enabled me to put together an interesting record of the history of Ashford and to build up a substantial photographic collection.

I am overwhelmed by the continued support for and huge success of *Changing Ashford*, *Ashford Then and Now* and *Ashford 1950–1980*. I am also very grateful to all those who have followed my fortunes over the past twenty-two years. Without their kindness, this book wouldn't be possible. As always, I have received much generosity from individuals and organisations that have readily allowed me to use their pictures. I would therefore like to give special thanks to the following:

Richard Filmer and Pauline Cooper, Halifax estate agents; James Adams; Jon Barrett; Terry Woodcock; photographer Jim Ashby and Mrs Joan Ashby; Howard and Christine Green; Alan and Lynn Ward; Cllr Rita Hawes; Peter and Pam Goodwin; Leo Whitlock, editor of the *Kentish Express*, Ashford edition; Mike Bennett, Sarah Linney, Dave Downey, Barry Hollis, Gary Browne and all at the Kent Messenger Group; Ben Grabham, Ray Wilkinson and Pam Herrapath at Ashford Borough Council; Julia Taylor and all at Kent Regional Newspapers; Nigel Taylor and the staff at Waterstones; Nick Kington and the staff at WH Smith; Maureen Apps and the staff at Sussex Stationers; Massimo and Mauro Deidda; David 'Taffy' James at Charter House (Berkeley Estates); Betty Shadwell; Brenda and George Sharp; the late Tom Hall and his wife Mollie; Debbie Saunders at the Centre for Kentish Studies; the late Walter Briscall; Emma Keeler, Joy Pritchard and Fiona Hukins, Kent Arts and Libraries, Ashford; Cllr Allen and Mrs Christine Wells; Cllr Bob and Mrs Daphne Davidson; Chris Mawson and Donna Geeves at Simmons Aerofilms; the Towers School; Richard Stafford, Colyer Commercial; Lyn Sumner; Gloria Lavender; Jenny Marshall; Sylvia Marsh; Kevin, Paula, Stephanie and Rob at Snappy Snaps, Ashford; Lucinda Walker at English Heritage.

As chairman of the recently established Ashford History Forum I would like also to express my thanks and gratitude to David Geoghegan at Kent County Council and to County Councillors Elizabeth Tweed, George Koowaree and Derek Smyth for their monetary contribution towards this publication and the future works of the forum. Their generosity is very much appreciated. Also I owe a big thank-you to Martin Bacon, managing director of Ashford's Future Delivery Board and Angie Plowman at Kent Community Foundation for their continued support.

I also owe thanks to Ian and Sue Gambrill, who have kindly continued to allow me to use their pictures. Since my last book went to press, Ian and Sue have sold their commercial photography business to Martin Apps, who continues to excel with Countrywide, and Sue has created Reflections Images Past and Present using both the Weavers and Countrywide images to create a 200,000-plus photo library dating back to 1949. I wish Ian and Sue the best of luck with their new venture. The pictures are fantastic.

Thanks are also due to anyone whose name has not been acknowledged here, either through an oversight or because the original source or present ownership of pictures is unknown or unavailable.

And lastly, as always I owe thanks to Simon Fletcher, Michelle Tilling and Anne Bennett at Sutton Publishing.